SCIENCE MASTERS

MIXING AND MEASURING MATTER

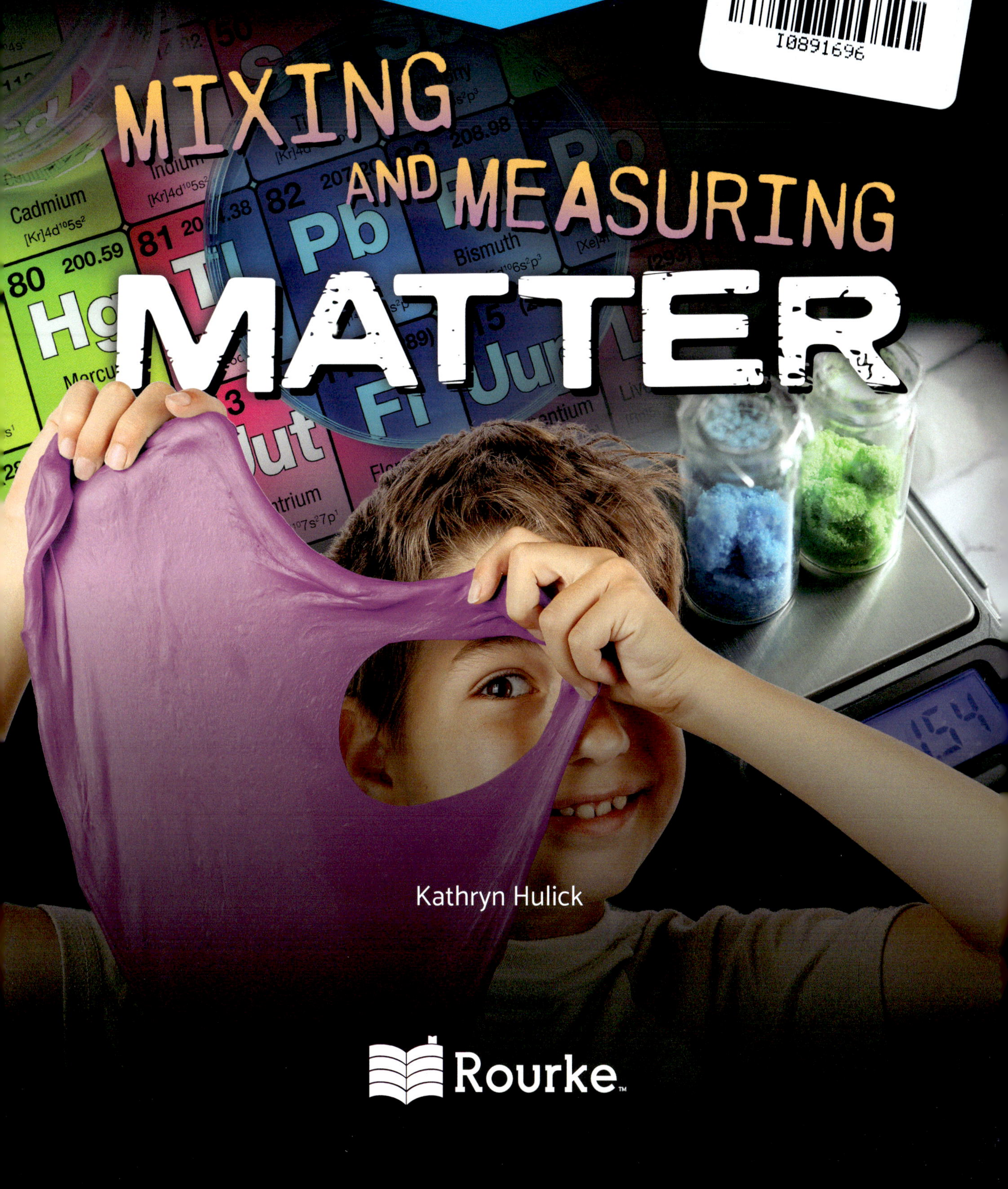

Kathryn Hulick

Rourke

ROURKE'S
SCHOOL to HOME
CONNECTIONS

BEFORE AND DURING READING ACTIVITIES

Before Reading: *Building Background Knowledge and Vocabulary*

Building background knowledge can help children process new information and build upon what they already know. Before reading a book, it is important to tap into what children already know about the topic. This will help them develop their vocabulary and increase their reading comprehension.

Questions and Activities to Build Background Knowledge:

1. Look at the front cover of the book and read the title. What do you think this book will be about?
2. What do you already know about this topic?
3. Take a book walk and skim the pages. Look at the table of contents, photographs, captions, and bold words. Did these text features give you any information or predictions about what you will read in this book?

Vocabulary: *Vocabulary Is Key to Reading Comprehension*

Use the following directions to prompt a conversation about each word.

- Read the vocabulary words.
- What comes to mind when you see each word?
- What do you think each word means?

Vocabulary Words:

- *chemical reactions*
- *compounds*
- *heterogeneous*
- *homogeneous*
- *mixtures*
- *molecules*
- *nuclear reactions*
- *properties*
- *proportions*
- *rigid*
- *synthetic*
- *vibrate*

During Reading: *Reading for Meaning and Understanding*

To achieve deep comprehension of a book, children are encouraged to use close reading strategies. During reading, it is important to have children stop and make connections. These connections result in deeper analysis and understanding of a book.

Close Reading a Text

During reading, have children stop and talk about the following:

- Any confusing parts
- Any unknown words
- Text to text, text to self, text to world connections
- The main idea in each chapter or heading

Encourage children to use context clues to determine the meaning of any unknown words. These strategies will help children learn to analyze the text more thoroughly as they read.

When you are finished reading this book, turn to the next-to-last page for **Text-Dependent Questions** and an **Extension Activity**.

TABLE OF CONTENTS

CHAPTER ONE

TINY BUILDING BLOCKS

Look at the stuff around you. Light bulbs, snow, ice cream, slime, you name it. It's all made of matter. When a light glows, when ice cream melts, when slime oozes, or when any other stuff in the universe changes, energy is at work. Together, matter and energy make up everything we experience.

Energy in the form of heat causes matter to change. It determines whether rain or snow will fall, or whether your ice cream is a cool treat or a sticky mess.

All matter is made up of the same building blocks. These are called *atoms*. Atoms are too small to see with your eyes. A single speck of dust may contain trillions of them!

A single atom is very small–about one-tenth of a billionth of a meter across.

Albert Einstein
1879–1955

Einstein's Equation

Matter and energy can change into each other. Physicist Albert Einstein's famous equation $E=mc^2$ *means that a very small amount of matter contains a huge amount of energy.*

Jelly beans, bricks, ice, and many other things in our daily lives seem still and solid. Yet atoms **vibrate** constantly. And they contain mostly empty space. In the very center of an atom sits the *nucleus*. It's made of tiny particles called *protons* and *neutrons*. Very far away, even tinier particles called *electrons* zip around. If the nucleus were the size of a peanut, the entire atom would be the size of a sports stadium!

Despite all this empty space, our bodies don't flow through walls or fall apart. Why? Those electrons act like the blades of a spinning fan. They seem to be everywhere at once. They can push other atoms away or grab on and hold tight.

ELECTRON CLOUD MODEL

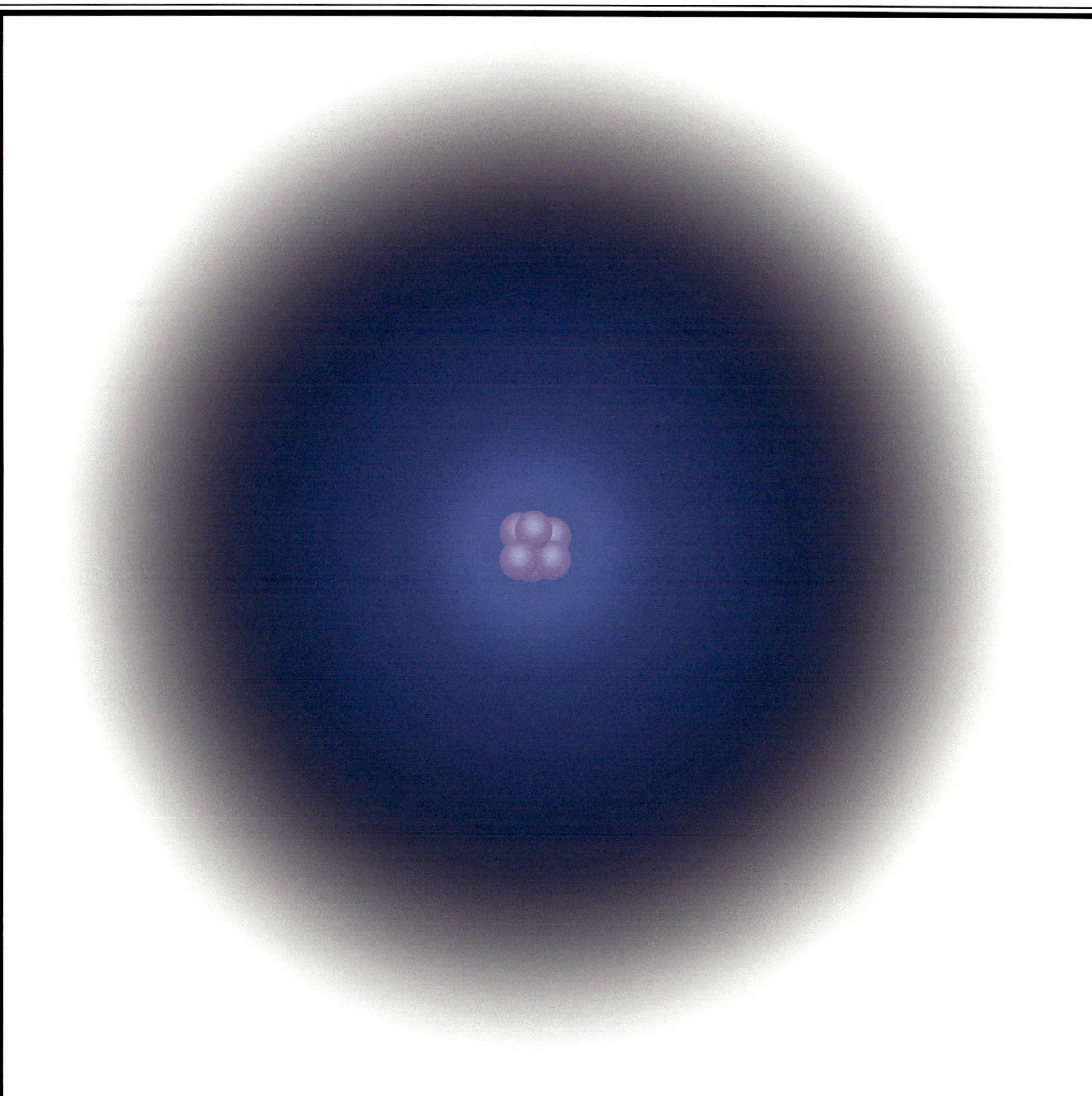

This model of an atom shows the nucleus at the center of a cloud of moving electrons. Since the exact paths of electrons is unknown, the cloud shows the most probable positions of electrons in an atom.

Atoms almost never float around alone. They usually link together to form **molecules**. The atoms inside a molecule share electrons.

Helium gas has two protons in each atom. Its atomic symbol is He.

Atoms come in many different types. These types are called the elements. Each has a different number of protons in its nucleus. The helium in a balloon and the gold in a ring are two examples of elements.

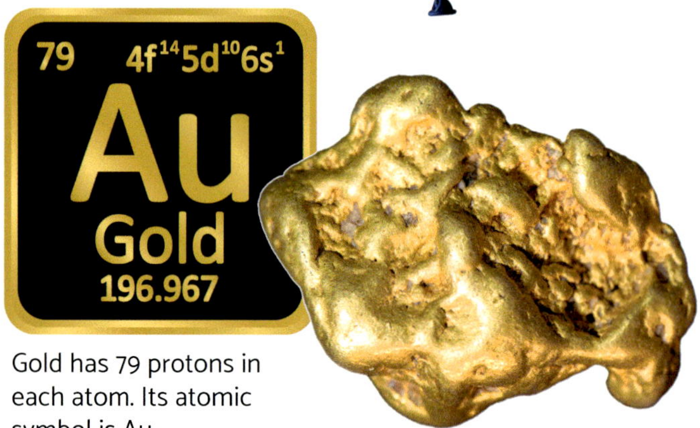

Gold has 79 protons in each atom. Its atomic symbol is Au.

Molecules called **compounds** contain atoms of more than one element. For example, a water molecule, H_2O, forms from two atoms of hydrogen and one atom of oxygen. A molecule of salt is another compound.

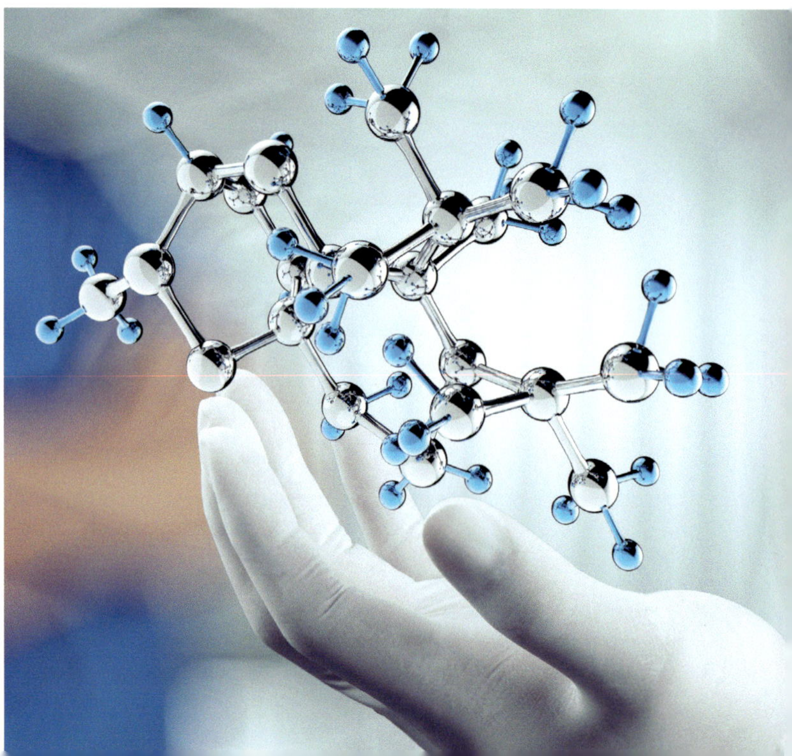

In this model of a molecule, each clear circle represents the nucleus of an atom. The blue circles are electrons.

How Many Elements?

Ninety-eight elements exist naturally on Earth. People have also created new elements in the lab, all the way up to number 118. Most of these quickly break apart into smaller elements.

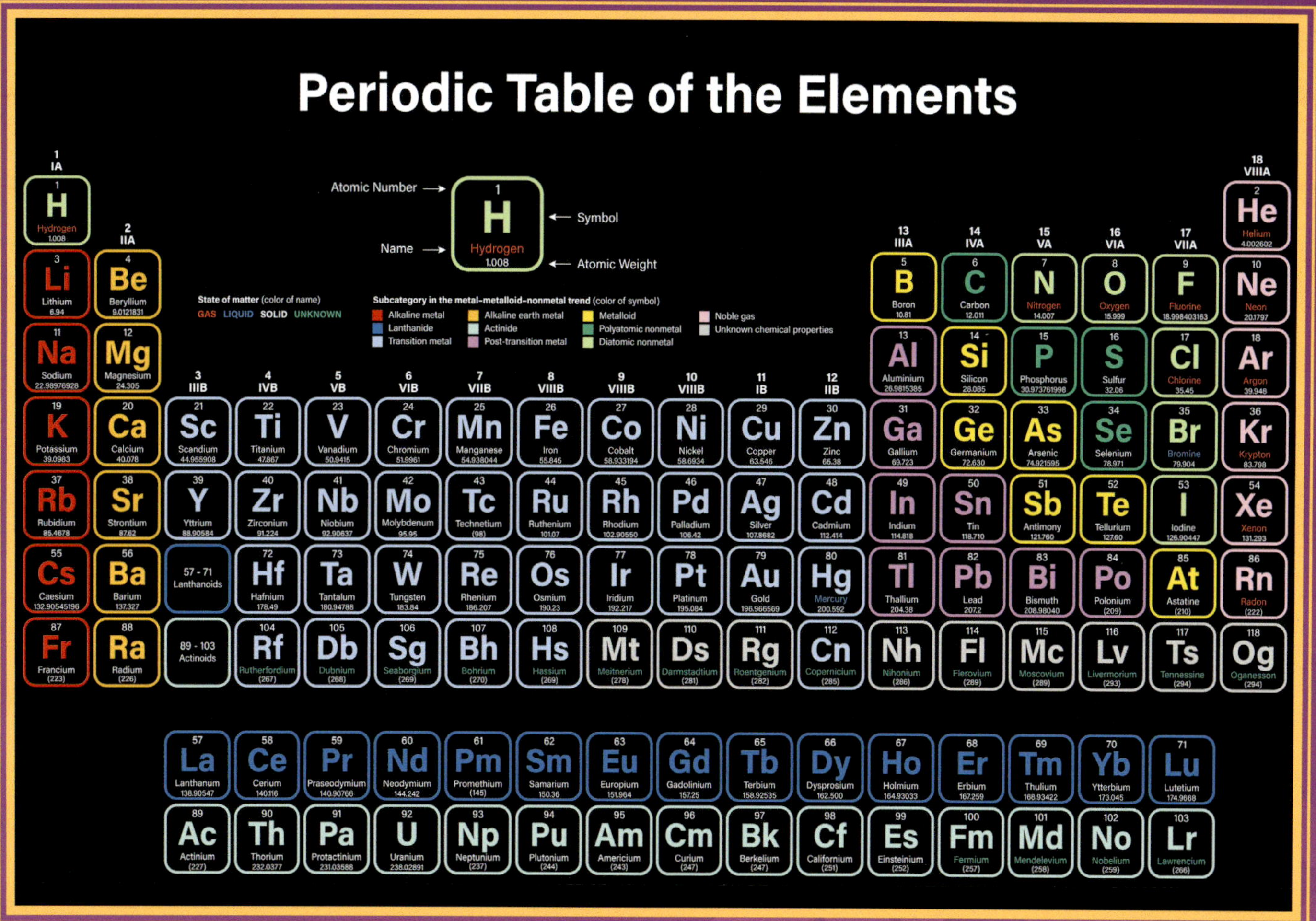

Magma that bursts from a volcano usually contains molecules of rock called *silicate*. Atoms of silicon and oxygen make up each silicate molecule.

The same elements make up all of the stuff on Earth and in the rest of the universe. So how can things as vastly different as balloons and jelly beans and volcanoes all exist? When atoms join into molecules, they form a certain material. This material looks and acts differently than any of the elements alone. It has different **properties**.

For example, water is wet and shiny. But if you could break apart all of the molecules in a glass of water, you'd end up with hydrogen and oxygen atoms. Pure hydrogen and oxygen are both invisible gases. They look very different than water.

Properties of matter include color, shape, hardness, and the ability to conduct electricity. We use properties to tell materials apart.

Each water molecule contains two hydrogen atoms and one oxygen atom.

CHAPTER TWO

TAKING UP SPACE

Matter has three especially important properties. The first important property is mass. Mass is how much of a substance exists. You may not know your own mass. But you probably know how much you weigh. Weight is the effect of gravity on a certain mass of matter.

Earth's gravity pulls people, tomatoes, and other objects toward the ground.

If you weigh 100 pounds (45 kilograms) on Earth, then you'd weigh just 17 pounds (8 kilograms) on the moon.

Moon Jump

If you traveled to the moon, your mass would stay the same. But you would weigh much less because the pull of gravity is lower on the moon. You would be able to jump around ten feet (three meters) into the air!

The second important property of matter is volume. Volume is how much space a mass of matter takes up. Imagine that you have to carry ten pounds (4.5 kilograms) of bricks or feathers. Both loads weigh the same. But the bricks fit into a small box. The feathers take up much more space, so they are more awkward to carry.

The United States Postal Service charges extra to ship heavy packages. It also charges more for very large, bulky packages—even if these packages don't weigh much.

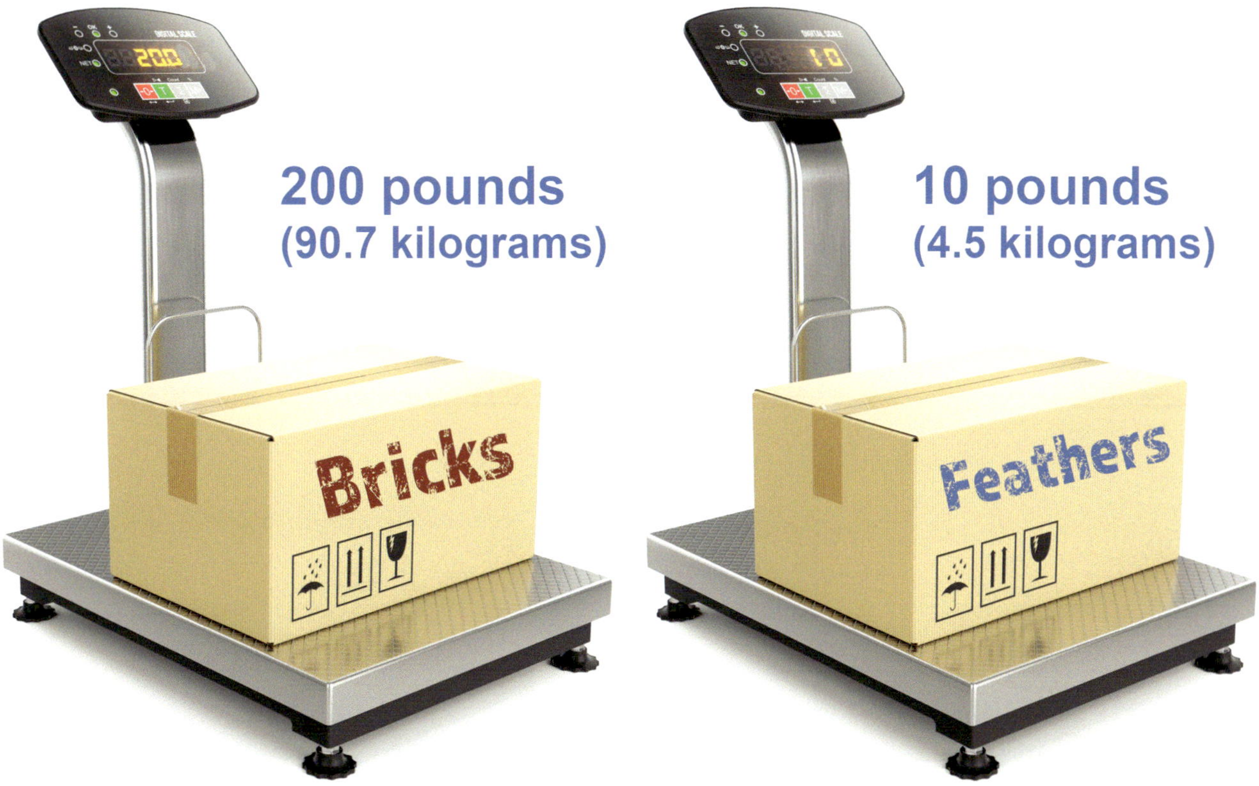

The matter in bricks is packed tightly together. The matter in a feather is spread out, leaving lots of space for air.

However, if you had to carry either bricks or feathers in boxes of the same size, you'd pick the feathers. That's because of the third important property of matter, density. Density describes how closely a mass of matter squishes together within a space. Very dense things, like bricks, weigh more than the same volume of something less dense, like feathers.

This scientist measures an object's height. She will use centimeters as her units.

When scientists want to know the mass, weight, volume, or density of matter, they take measurements. They also measure many other properties of matter, including temperature and length. Measuring matter is a part of daily life. Whenever you check the weather, figure out your shoe size, or step on a scale, you are measuring something.

Measurements only make sense if you use the right units. In the United States, people use pounds for weight and gallons for volume. But scientists and most of the rest of the people in the world use kilograms and liters. Understanding units allows you to compare your measurements to ones that other people have made.

Units Matter!

Seventy pounds (32 kilograms) is the average weight of a ten-year-old child. But 70 kilograms (154 pounds) is the average weight of an adult man. And 70 tons (63.5 metric tons) is the weight of a right whale!

Kitchen measuring cups may be labeled with both standard and metric units.

CHAPTER THREE

CHANGING FORM

Have you ever put an ice cube into your mouth and felt the cold, hard ice melt into water? Or maybe you've watched misty steam rise from a pot of boiling water. Ice, steam, and liquid water are all made of H_2O molecules. But they have very different properties. That's because the way molecules fit together can change.

The steam that rises from a cooking pot is water in its gas form.

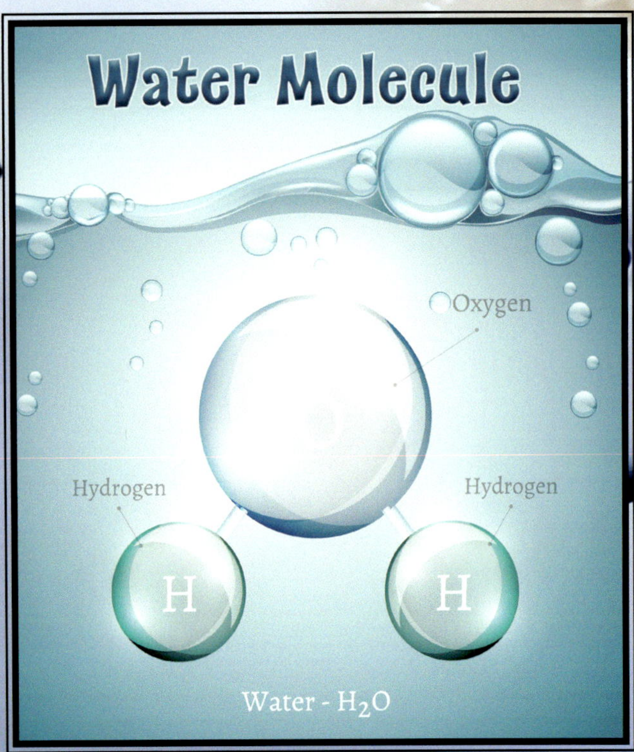

A melting ice cube is changing from a solid to a liquid.

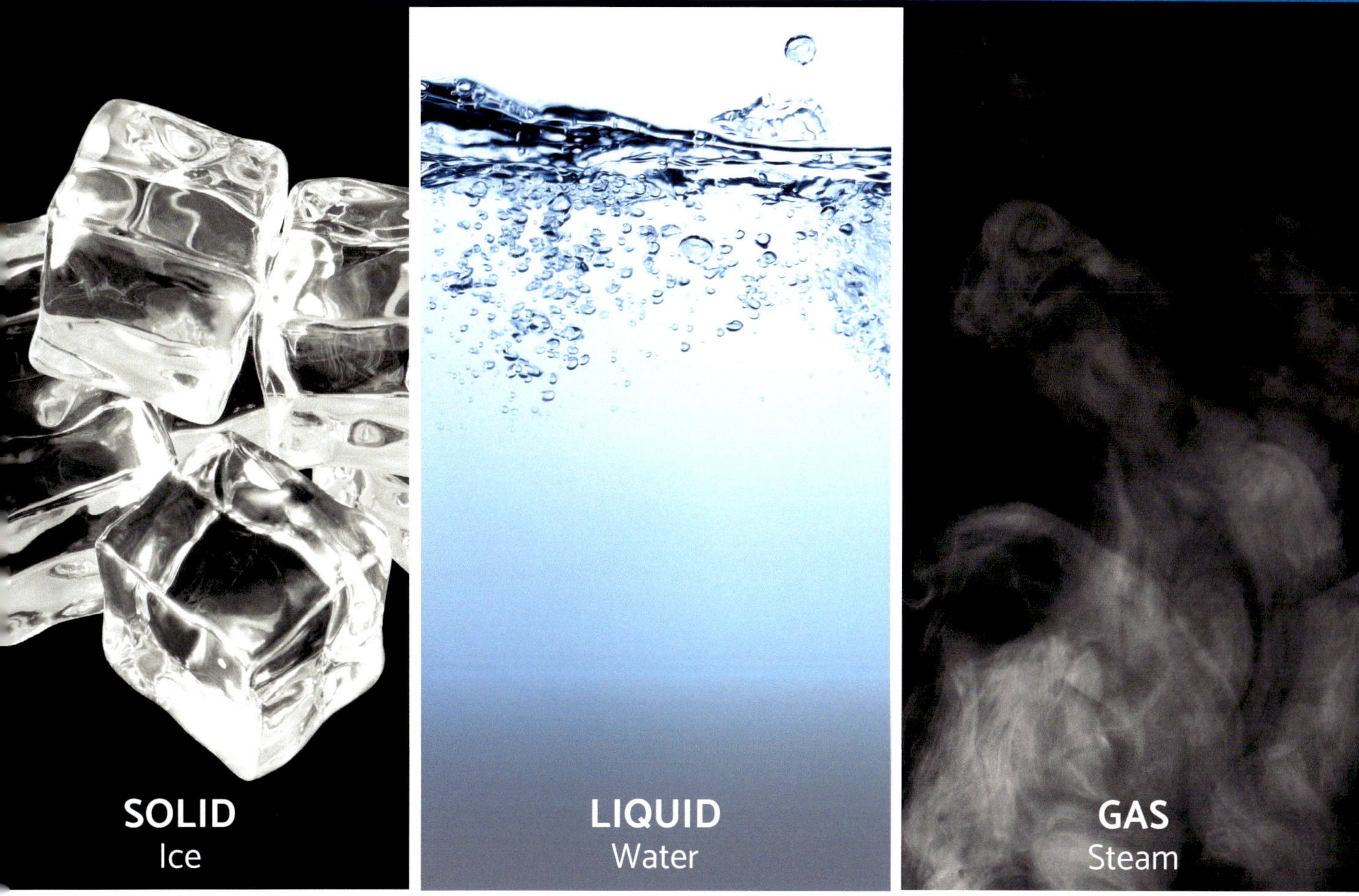

When molecules pack tightly together into a **rigid** structure, they form a solid, like ice. When molecules slip and slide around, they form a liquid, like water. And when molecules bounce around freely to fill whatever container they are in, they form a gas, like the vapor in clouds.

Why Ice Cubes Float

Most of the time, when something turns solid, its molecules squeeze more closely together. But when water freezes, the molecules form a special crystal structure with extra space in between molecules. This makes ice less dense than water. So, it floats!

The sun's energy changes solid ice into liquid water.

Heat and cold can make matter change form. An icicle melts in the hot sun. Liquid magma running down the side of a volcano cools into solid rock. Temperature is a measurement of how quickly the molecules in a substance are moving. As temperature rises, molecules move faster. They may get moving so quickly that they can't hold together anymore. Then, the matter changes to a liquid or gas form. In the same way, as temperature drops, molecules slow down into a more rigid state.

The inside of Earth is so hot that rocks melt. After a volcano spews out these hot, liquid rocks, they cool into a solid.

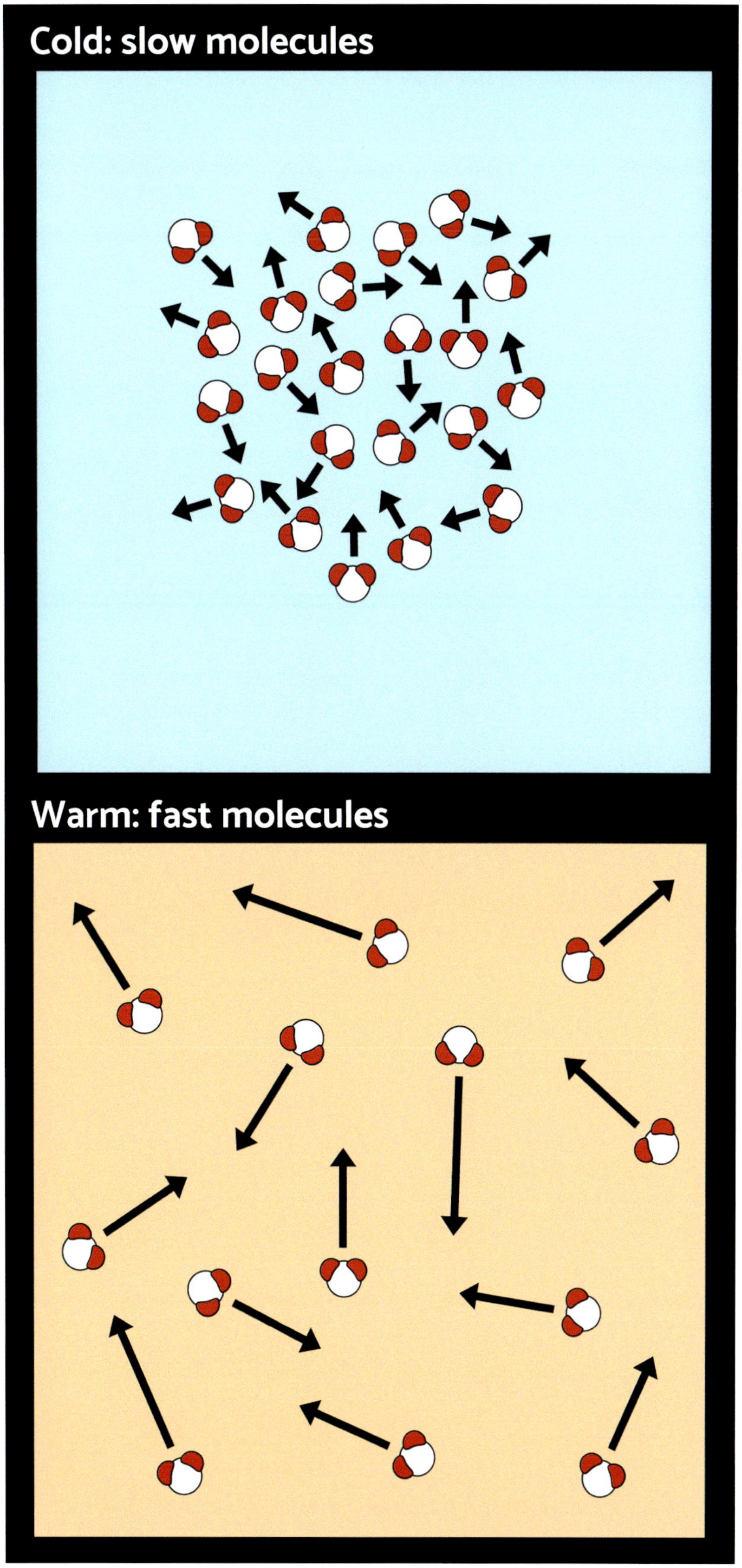
Cold: slow molecules
Warm: fast molecules

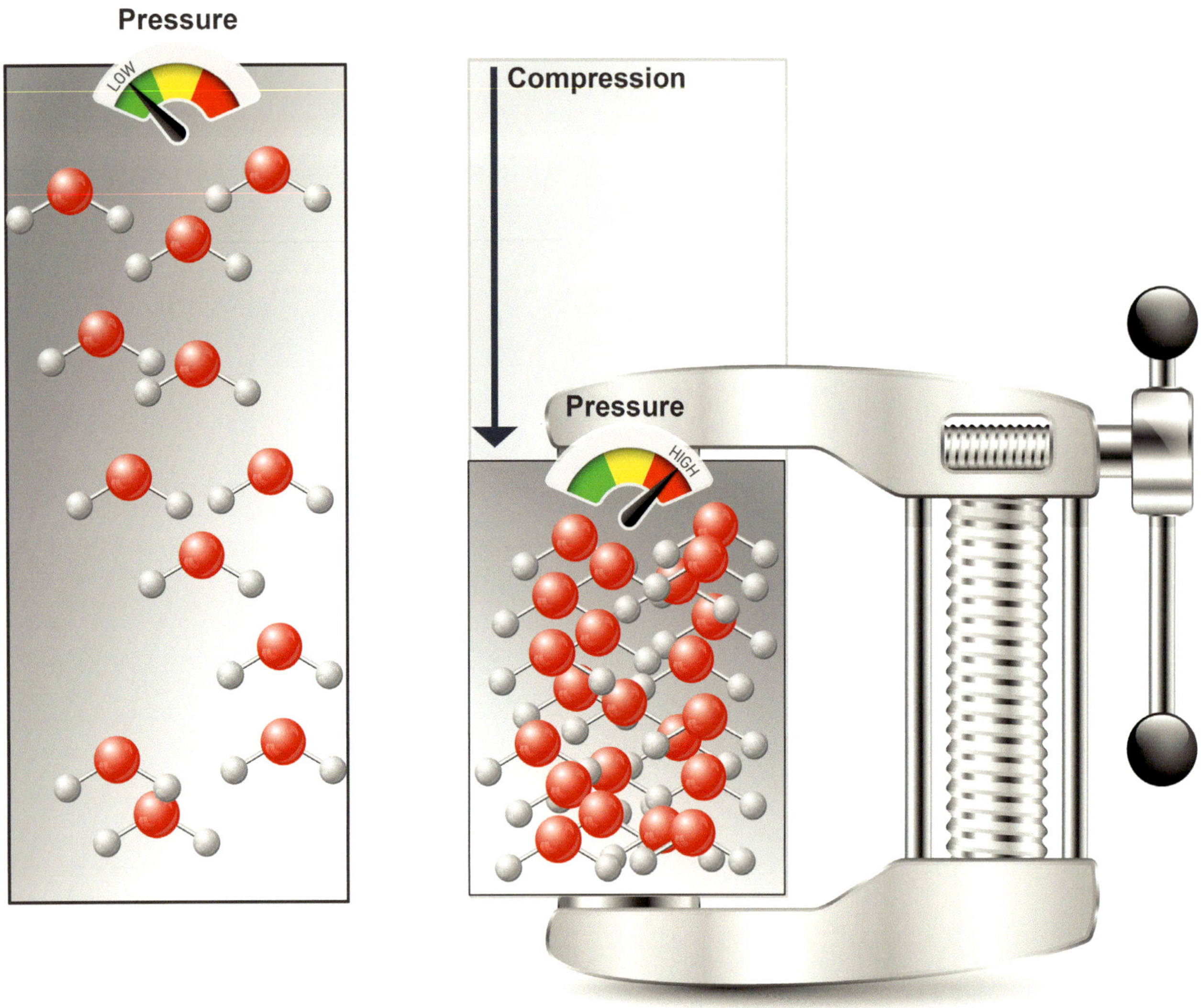

Under low pressure, molecules move freely. Under high pressure, they get forced closer together.

Changes in pressure also make a difference in matter. Pressure is the amount of force pushing on an area. Adding pressure squishes molecules closer together into a more rigid structure.

On Earth, all of the air in the atmosphere presses down on the ground. Up high in the mountains, less air presses down, so the air pressure is lower. This makes it easier for molecules to move around.

Some people have trouble breathing at high altitudes. The low pressure means that fewer molecules of air enter the body with each breath.

Want to Make Some Tea?

High in the mountains, water boils faster. The air pressure is lower there. So, water boils and turns to steam at a lower temperature. In fact, if the pressure gets low enough, water will boil at room temperature!

All types of matter can change to a solid, a liquid, or a gas state. But you need the right combination of temperature and pressure. Some types of matter will only change at extreme temperatures or pressures. These conditions may not happen naturally on Earth.

Dry ice is frozen carbon dioxide. It changes directly from a solid into a gas.

Alien Seas

Methane is the main ingredient in natural gas. On Earth, people use this gas for heating and cooking. But on Saturn's moon Titan, the temperature is so frigid that methane forms liquid seas.

The methane seas on Titan appear orange.

A fourth state of matter also exists. It is called *plasma*. It forms at extremely hot temperatures. The sun and other stars are made of plasma. Lightning and neon signs contain plasma. In this state, the nucleus and electrons in each atom have separated.

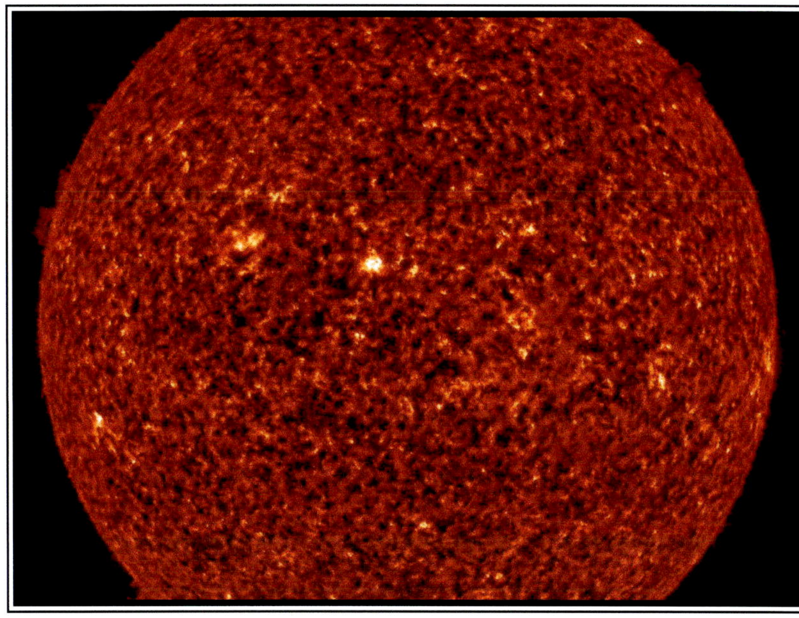

Our sun is mostly made up of hydrogen and helium in their plasma forms.

Electricity turns the gas inside a neon sign into glowing plasma.

CHAPTER FOUR

MIX IT UP

There is no such thing as a lemonade atom or a mud molecule. Most of the things in our daily lives are not pure elements or compounds. They are **mixtures**.

What do you get when you mix water, lemons, and sugar? A nice, refreshing glass of lemonade!

Silver is a soft metal. Mixing in copper or other metals creates sterling silver, a harder, stronger material.

Mixtures contain several substances jumbled together. Sometimes, the substances mix together evenly. In lemonade, every part of the drink contains the same **proportions** of sugar, water, and lemon juice. Air contains different gases, all mixed evenly. And the sterling silver in a fancy ring contains silver and other metals, evenly mixed. These are all **homogeneous** mixtures.

Other mixtures contain clumps or layers of different substances. These are **heterogeneous** mixtures. Mud is water mixed with clumps of sand, dirt, bugs, and more. Pizza has layers of cheese and toppings.

A Sandy Puzzle

Is the sand on a beach evenly mixed? Two piles of sand may look identical. But look more closely and you'll see a slightly different mix of rocks and bits of shell in every handful.

What are shells made of? Molecules of calcium carbonate were secreted from the body of a mollusk before hardening into a protective covering.

All mixtures have one thing in common. You can separate them to get the original ingredients back. Dragging a net through a swimming pool removes debris mixed into the water. You can also easily pick pretty shells or rocks out of sand.

A metallurgist is someone who knows how to mix and separate metals.

Sometimes, separating a mixture isn't so easy. To get the sugar out of lemonade, you can boil the drink. The water will turn to steam, and the sugar will stay behind. Heating sterling silver to the right temperature will melt the silver but leave other metals solid. After separating a mixture, you'll always have the same total amount of mass that you started with.

Panning for Gold

Sometimes, the mud at the bottom of a river contains flecks of gold. To get the gold out, prospectors put the mud into a pan with water. Then, they spin the pan around. Gold is heavier than rocks. So, it settles near the middle of the pan while lighter rocks get flung to the edges.

Gold is a dense, heavy metal.

CHAPTER FIVE

READY, SET, REACT!

Have you ever made pancakes? First, you stir together the dry ingredients. At this point, you have a mixture in your bowl. If you had the right tools, you could separate out the flour, baking powder, and salt. But then you stir in milk, and something interesting happens. The molecules of milk and baking powder break apart. This releases water, bubbles of gas, and other new substances.

Some pancake ingredients form a mixture.

Other ingredients make changes start to happen.

When you drop pancake batter onto a hot pan, the changes continue. The heat breaks apart more molecules. The freed atoms join into new molecules. These **chemical reactions** transform the gooey batter into a soft, delicious pancake.

The bubbles in pancake batter are pockets of gas that broke free from other molecules.

In a cooked pancake, the original ingredients have transformed into new molecules. Yum!

Chemical reactions happen all around us. In a burning campfire, a bursting firework, or on a rusting bicycle, molecules break and join. Reactions even happen inside us! Your stomach specializes in breaking up food molecules.

As wood heats, its molecules begin to break apart. When these pieces meet oxygen from the air, flames blaze. This produces more heat and breaks more molecules.

How do you know if a chemical reaction happened? It takes energy to break molecules. And energy gets let out when atoms join. Clues that energy has been absorbed or released include heat, light, smells, sounds, or color changes.

Does something stink? A gross or delicious smell is a big clue that a chemical reaction is taking place.

Rotting is a chemical reaction that you can detect by color changes, texture changes, and gross smells.

After a chemical reaction, you can't get the original ingredients back again. Those substances are gone. But their atoms all still exist. Matter can never appear or disappear. Neither can energy. But both matter and energy can change.

Not all color changes indicate a chemical reaction. Mixing blue and yellow paint makes green. But the molecules of the blue and green paints have not changed.

A log in a campfire seems to disappear as it burns up. In fact, all of the matter inside the log becomes gas, smoke, and ashes. And chemical energy stored in the log becomes heat energy in the flames.

The logs in this fire didn't disappear. Their molecules drifted away as gas and smoke.

Another type of reaction breaks apart atoms or joins them together. In these **nuclear reactions**, a tiny amount of matter transforms into a huge amount of energy. These powerful reactions keep the sun shining. They also allow nuclear power plants to make a lot of electricity from a tiny amount of fuel.

A nuclear reaction called *fusion* melds atoms together inside our sun.

At nuclear power plants, atoms get broken apart in *fission* reactions. The plant turns energy from these reactions into electricity.

Each star in a galaxy is like a factory churning out the elements on the periodic table.

We Are Stardust

The atoms that make up our bodies, along with all the stuff on Earth, formed inside of stars. The intense heat and pressure inside a star forces light atoms to fuse together into larger, heavier atoms. This process created all of the different elements.

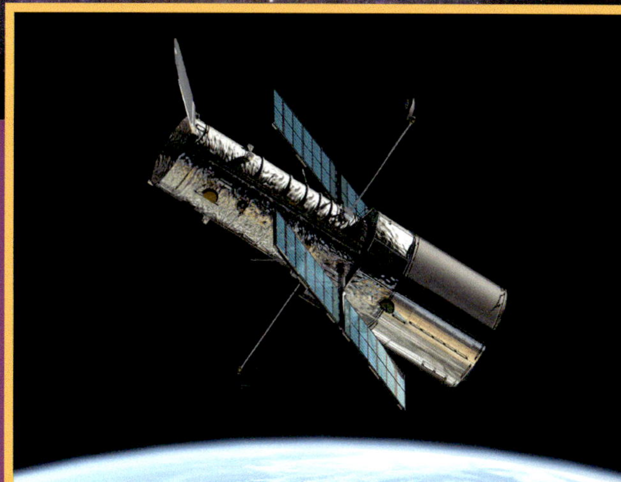

The Hubble Space Telescope helped reveal that the universe has around two trillion galaxies—each filled with billions of stars.

CHAPTER SIX

CHEMISTRY IN DAILY LIFE

Chemical reactions make life possible. Plants make their own food from sunlight using a chemical reaction called *photosynthesis*. Animals' bodies use chemical reactions to get energy out of the food they eat.

The photosynthesis reaction gives off oxygen that people breathe.

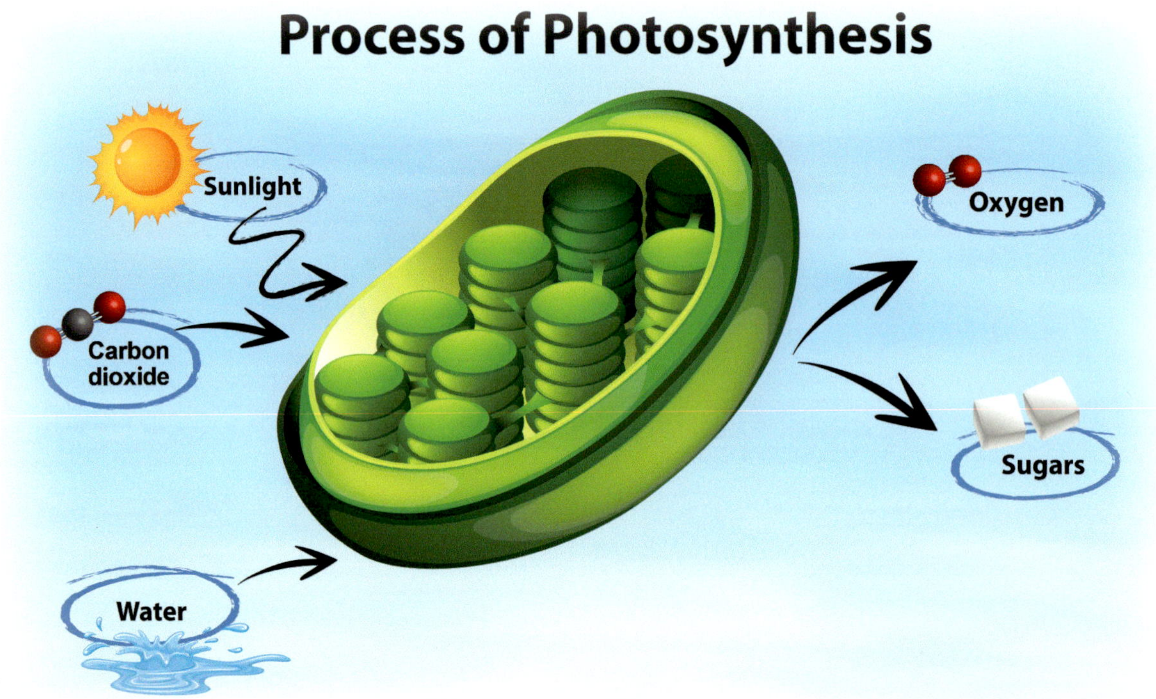

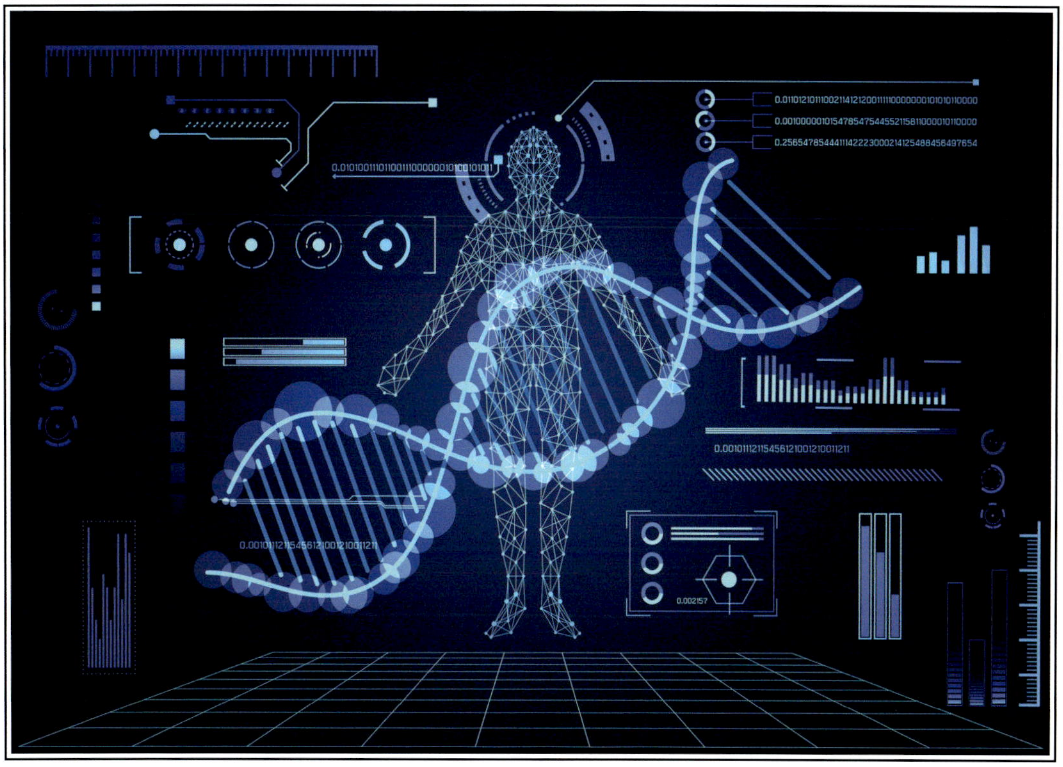

Chemicals also carry messages throughout your body. As you think, quintillions—billions of billions—of chemical reactions cascade through your brain.

Whodunnit?

Fingertips leave behind oil and sweat. Police use substances that react to the oil and sweat to collect fingerprints. They also use chemical reactions to identify people from traces of DNA.

Plastic does not exist in nature. Its molecules are manufactured in factories.

Humans have harnessed the power of chemical reactions. We have invented many new materials that do not exist in nature. These are called **synthetic** materials.

Chemicals inside a battery react to produce electricity. When the chemicals run out, the battery dies.

Oil found naturally under the ground gets transformed into many synthetic products. These include plastics and gasoline. Chemists also craft new medicines and foods in labs.

Knowledge of chemistry gives people power over matter and energy. Without chemistry, we wouldn't be able to cook. We wouldn't be able to construct cities or power our homes and electronics. Chemistry allows us to change matter and energy into the shapes and forms that we need. It allows us to transform our world.

ACTIVITY

MIXTURE OR REACTION?

Can you tell the difference between a mixture and a chemical reaction? Follow the instructions below to make two different substances. Which one shows signs of molecules breaking or joining? That one is the chemical reaction. Common clues include heat, light, smells, sounds, or color changes.

Important: Make sure you have an adult's permission and supervision.

Supplies

- cornstarch
- measuring cups and spoons
- 2 small bowls
- water
- spoon
- safety glasses
- iodine
- eyedropper

Directions

Part 1:

1. Put one cup (125 grams) of cornstarch into a small bowl.

2. Slowly add $\frac{1}{2}$ cup (120 milliliters) of water, stirring with a spoon or mixing with your fingers until the substance gets gooey. You may not need to use all of the water.

3. The goo is called *oobleck*. Play with it and notice its properties.

4. Leave your oobleck sitting in the bowl for a few days without touching it. What happens? Is this change evidence that oobleck is a mixture or the product of a chemical reaction?

Part 2:

1. Pour one cup (240 milliliters) of water into the other bowl.

2. Add two tablespoons (30 grams) of cornstarch and stir until it dissolves.

3. Put on safety glasses. Carefully fill the eyedropper with iodine.

4. Add 10 to 20 drops of iodine to the bowl, one at a time, until you see a change.

5. How did the solution change? Do you think a chemical reaction happened? Why or why not?

Glossary

chemical reactions (KEM-i-kuhl ree-AK-shuhnz): changes that break apart molecules or join atoms to form molecules

compounds (KAHM-poundz): substances, such as salt or water, made from two or more chemical elements

heterogeneous (he-tuh-ruh-JEE-nee-uhs): unevenly mixed or containing parts that are very different

homogeneous (hoh-muh-JEE-nee-uhs): evenly mixed or containing parts that are all similar

mixtures (MIKS-churz): portions of matter that contain two or more substances that retain or keep their own properties

molecules (MAH-luh-kyoolz): groups of atoms linked together; the smallest units that a chemical compound can be divided into that still display all of its chemical properties

nuclear reactions (NOO-klee-ur ree-AK-shuhnz): changes that break apart atoms or join particles to form atoms

properties (PRAH-pur-teez): qualities or characteristics of things, such as size, shape, color, or texture

proportions (pruh-POR-shuhnz): relationships between different parts of a whole

rigid (RIJ-id): stiff, fixed, and difficult to move or bend; arranged in a tight structure

synthetic (sin-THE-tik): artificial; made in a lab rather than in nature

vibrate (VYE-brate): to shake or quiver in steady motion

Index

Text-Dependent Questions

1. What particles are found inside an atom?
2. What are five properties of matter?
3. How do temperature and pressure affect matter?
4. What happens to molecules during a chemical reaction?
5. What are two synthetic materials that humans invented?

Extension Activity

Help a parent or other adult cook a meal. What parts of the recipe use mixtures? Do any chemical reactions occur? How do they change the food? Research the answers to these questions and teach your adult cooking partner about the chemistry of your meal.

About the Author

Kathryn Hulick decided to write books for kids after returning from two years serving in the Peace Corps in Kyrgyzstan. Her favorite subjects are science and technology. She's written about everything from robots and outer space to dinosaurs. She enjoys hiking, painting, reading, and working in her garden. Learn more about her work at kathrynhulick.com.

www.rourkebooks.com

PHOTO CREDITS: Cover photos: kid holding slime © andras_csontos, substances on a scale © Ihor Matsiievskyi, periodic table © Victor Moussa (all cover images from Shutterstock.com); Page 4-5: istock.com | Evgenij84, istock.com | nito100, istock.com | zoom-zoom, 5464893 ©Naci Yavuz | Dreamstime.com; Page 6-7: istock.com | daniel_wiedemann, Shutterstock.com | extender_01. Page 8-9: istock.com | everythingpossible, 114092216 © Konstantin Semenov | Dreamstime.com, istock.com | MarcelC, 113826052 ©Konstantin Semenov | Dreamstime.com, istock.com | alekcey, istock.com | duntaro; Page 10-11: istock.com | TrueCapture, istock.com | orinoco-art, istock.com | petrroudny, istock.com | Udomsook; Page 12-13: istock.com | Voyagerix, istock.com | saje, istock.com | AndreyPopov/78570861, istock.com | hkeita; Page 14-15: istock.com | -slav-, istock.com | Rostislav_Sedlacek, istock.com | Grassetto; Page 16-17: istock.com | atomm, istock.com | schulzie, istock.com | STUDIOGRANDOUEST, istock.com | Rena-Marie, istock.com | weerapatkiatdumrong; Page 18-19: istock.com | AnnaElizabethPhotography, Shutterstock.com | robert_s, istock.com | newannyart, istock.com | silverjohn, istock.com | Hyzop, istock.com | kuppa_rock; Page 20-21: istock.com | Leonid Ikan, istock.com | namenoname, 120057315 ©OSweetNature | Dreamstime.com; Page 22-23: istock.com | SergeiKorolko, istock.com | chromatos, istock.com | pialhovik. ©BDPub, istock.com | Willard; Page 24-25: Shutterstock | FOTOGRIN, ©NASA/JPL, istock.com | VTT Studio, ©NASA/JPL; Page 26-27: istock.com | margouillatphotos, istock.com | choness, istock.com | Hyrma, istock.com | Boonchuay1970, istock.con | Cristiano Babini; Page 28-29: istock.com | kurapy11, istock.com | mis1il, istock.com | Yulia Buzaeva; Page 30-31: istock.com | Osobystist, istock.com | dima_sidelnikov, istock.com | Luftklick; Page 32-33: istock.com | SStajic, istock.com | Stanislav Ostranitsa; Page 34-35: istock.com | KimberlyShavender, istock.com | bowie15, istock.com | margouillatphotos; Page 36-37: istock.com | Toltek, istock.com | Osobystist, istock.com | Richard Schafer; Page 38-39: istock.com | jotily, istock.com | raspirator, NASA/JPL, ESA/NASA; Page 40-41: istock.com | coffeekai, istock.com | colematt, 127461533 ©Nattapon Kongbunmee | Dreamstime.com, istock.com | everythingpossible; Page 42-43: istock.com | Yevhenii Orlov, istock.com | mipan, 10026204 ©Scanrail | Dreamstime.com, istock.com | gorodenkoff;

Edited by: Kim Thompson

Produced by Blue Door Education for Rourke Educational Media. Cover and interior design by: Jennifer Dydyk

Library of Congress PCN Data

Mixing and Measuring Matter / Kathryn Hulick
(Science Masters)
ISBN 978-1-73161-470-4 (hard cover)
ISBN 978-1-73161-277-9 (soft cover)
ISBN 978-1-73161-575-6 (e-Book)
ISBN 978-1-73161-680-7 (e-Pub)
Library of Congress Control Number: 2019932385

Rourke Educational Media
Printed in the United States of America
05-3162411973